T0379145

Joy to the World!

Christmas Around the Globe

written by
Kate DePalma

illustrated by
Sophie Fatus

It's almost Christmas! A bright time of year
For coming together with those we hold dear.

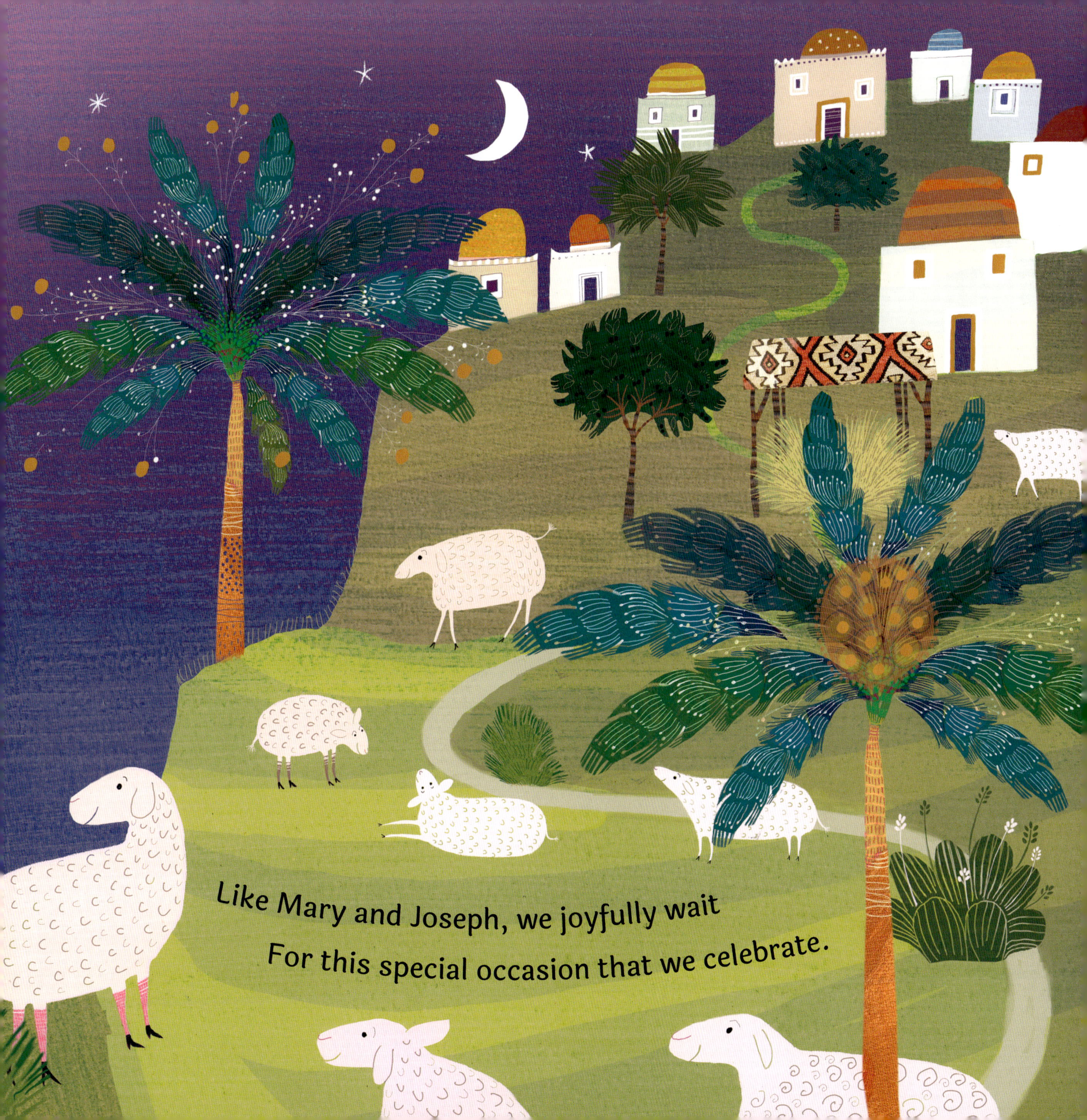

Like Mary and Joseph, we joyfully wait
For this special occasion that we celebrate.

The Christmas season in Colombia begins December 7 with a display of candles and lanterns called the **Day of Little Candles**.

We pray and make wishes as we light the lights,

Then all stroll together to take in the sights.

We make kuswar* for friends — cakes, pastries and tarts.
We're careful and quick. Making treats is an art.

*Pronounced KOOS-war

In India, Christmas is a time to gather together to make treats called **kuswar** to share with friends and family.

India

My pai fries the goodies and we roll the dough,
Then share them with family and people we know.

Simbang Gabi* stretches over nine days.
We wake up before dawn to worship and praise.

*Pronounced sim-BANG gah-BEE

Philippines
We come every day, and they say if you do,
Whatever you wish on day nine will come true.
During **Simbang Gabi** in the Philippines, Mass is
held at dawn for nine days leading up to Christmas.

Look at the snow! It's as cold as can be.
Let's stay in and decorate our Christmas tree.
Bringing an evergreen **Christmas tree** inside to decorate with ornaments and lights is an important part of the season in Canada.

Canada
The ornaments hung on the branches with care
Represent memories all of us share.

On Las Posadas* we put on a play
About Mary and Joseph, with nowhere to stay.

*Pronounced LAS poh-SAH-das

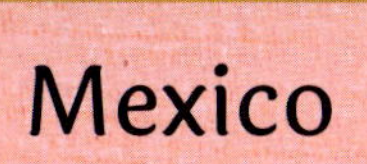

On one door each night, we knock and we sing,

Then all pray together for our newborn king.

During **Las Posadas**, people in Mexico act out the story of Mary and Joseph looking for a place to stay before Jesus was born.

In the time before Christmas, my family fasts.
We eat very simply. The days and weeks pass.

In Egypt, people fast from foods made from animal products for the weeks leading up to Christmas, and celebrate **breaking the fast** with a big meal.

Egypt
When Christmas Eve comes and the fasting time ends,
We eat zesty fattah* with family and friends.
*Pronounced FAH-tah

When it's Genna* and we're looking our best,
Sit down by the mesob† and you'll be impressed!
*Pronounced gen-NAH
† Pronounced MEH-sob
On **Genna**, Ethiopians break their Christmas season fast with a meal served on a basket-like table called a mesob.

When we start to eat, we all know what to do.
I'll feed you a bite, then you feed me one too!

A Christmas Day lit up with sizzling sun
Brings everyone out to the beach to have fun!

Australia

Grab a ball and a bat, and set up the wicket.
Such a hot summer day is just perfect for cricket.

Christmas comes in the summer in Australia, where the day is often spent at the **beach**, enjoying a picnic and playing cricket in the sunshine.

On Epiphany* night, we hang stockings and wait.
We know that the kind witch Befana† comes late.

*Pronounced eh-PIFF-eh-nee †Pronounced be-FAH-nah

Italy
Then "Viva, viva la Befana," we sing,
Excited to see all the goodies she'll bring.
Italian children look forward to an Epiphany night visit from **Befana**, a kind old woman who fills stockings with gifts.

Bring in the straw and we'll cover the floor.
Drop in some treats — then sprinkle some more!

On Christmas Eve in Serbia, adults pretend to be hens as they drop treats into **straw** spread on the ground, and children peep like chickens as they gather them!

The adults cluck like chickens and we peep, "Piju!"*
Let's pick up the goodies that our mama threw!

*Pronounced PEE-oo

On Christmas Eve, we have Mass at the church,
Then act out the story of Jesus's birth.

The festivities start late on **Noche Buena** in Argentina, where children act out the story of Christmas and then enjoy a midnight dinner with family.

Argentina
Our summery dinner is often served late.
We stay up past midnight! Can you stay awake?

Winter in Iceland brings Christmas Book Flood!
Let's go and pick gifts for the ones that we love.

The Christmas season in Iceland brings a **Christmas Book Flood**. Books are given as gifts, and enjoyed together on Christmas Eve after dinner.

Iceland
On Christmas Eve night, despite the cold weather,
We all exchange books and then read them together.

At Christmas, we build our Nativity scene:

A big rocky cave with fresh sprouts to add green.

Families create **Nativity scenes** in Lebanon, complete with fresh bean sprouts for greenery. A figure of Jesus is placed in the manger at midnight on Christmas Eve.

Lebanon

When Christmas Eve comes and we're filled with good cheer,
The scene is complete! Baby Jesus is here!

Though we might gather in different ways,
Christmas for many brings meaningful days.

Jesus is born! What a wonderful reason
For coming together for this sacred season.

What is Christmas?

Christmas is the celebration of the birth of Jesus in the Christian faith.

According to the Bible, a collection of texts holy to Christians, God sent an angel (a holy messenger) to a young woman named Mary, who was engaged to marry a man named Joseph. The angel told her she would become pregnant with a son named Jesus, who would be the son of God.

Mary was far from home in a town called Bethlehem when Jesus was born. There was no room at the guest house, or the inn, so Mary gave birth where the animals slept. They were visited by Wise Men (also called Magi) bearing gifts for the baby. The famous story of the birth of Baby Jesus, laid to rest in a manger of hay, surrounded by Mary and Joseph and farm animals, is called the Nativity.

Christmas is observed by billions of people around the world every year, usually on December 25.

The Day of Little Candles in Colombia

* Día de las velitas, the Day of Little Candles, is celebrated as a public holiday in Colombia on December 7. It marks the beginning of the Christmas season.
* Families light lanterns called faroles and small candles for Mary. These lights are placed on the streets, in windowsills, in parks and anywhere they can be seen.
* Because Colombia is in the southern half of the world, it is summertime at Christmas. In some parts of the country, candles are lit at dawn on the 7th after celebrating all night. Other places spend the day celebrating and wait until after the sun sets to light their candles.
* Many people walk through the cities, admiring the candles and festive decorations outside shops and homes. Duñuclo, a sweet fried dough, is a special treat during this time.

Making Kuswar in India

* Only about 2% of India's population celebrates Christmas, but some areas have a larger Christian population than others. Goa, a state on the southwest coast of India, is about 25% Christian.
* One popular Christmas tradition in Goa is making Christmas treats called kuswar to share. Families often gather to make the treats together. Children might learn the recipes from their mai or pai — their mother or father. Kidiyo (or kulkuls), curly pieces of fried dough dusted with sugar, are named for their shape — kidiyo means worm!
* On Christmas morning, many families have breakfast together and share kuswar with friends and loved ones.
* Religious services are an important part of the Christmas season in Goa, as well as creating Christmas cribs, also known as Nativity scenes. A figurine of the Baby Jesus is placed in the crib at midnight on Christmas Eve.

Simbang Gabi in the Philippines

* The nine religious services of Simbang Gabi begin at dawn on December 16 and end with a midnight service on Christmas Eve. Although the name means "night Mass," services are held at dawn so that people can attend Mass and still be rested for work.
* Communities celebrate with bright decorations, star-shaped paròl lanterns, and a belen, or Nativity scene. The paròls symbolize the star of Bethlehem that the Wise Men followed to find the Baby Jesus.
* If you attend all nine Simbang Gabi masses, it is thought that your Christmas wish will be granted.
* The Christmas season in the Philippines lasts for almost five months! It begins in September with early preparations and lasts through until the first weeks of January.

Christmas Trees in Canada

* In Canada, an evergreen tree makes the home ready for Christmas. Families decorate together using different ornaments and sparkling tinsel. Ornaments can represent memories. They can be handmade or be delicate works of art. Some families pass down ornaments from generation to generation.
* Eating treats like cookies and playing festive music makes decorating the tree a fun family activity. Some families hang stockings along the fireplace for Santa Claus, who is said to visit homes on Christmas Eve and leave gifts and treats in the stockings.
* Because they stay green all year, evergreens have been used as a symbol of everlasting life since ancient times. The tradition of bringing evergreens inside and decorating them for Christmas began hundreds of years ago in Europe. Today trees are a meaningful part of Christmas traditions around the world.

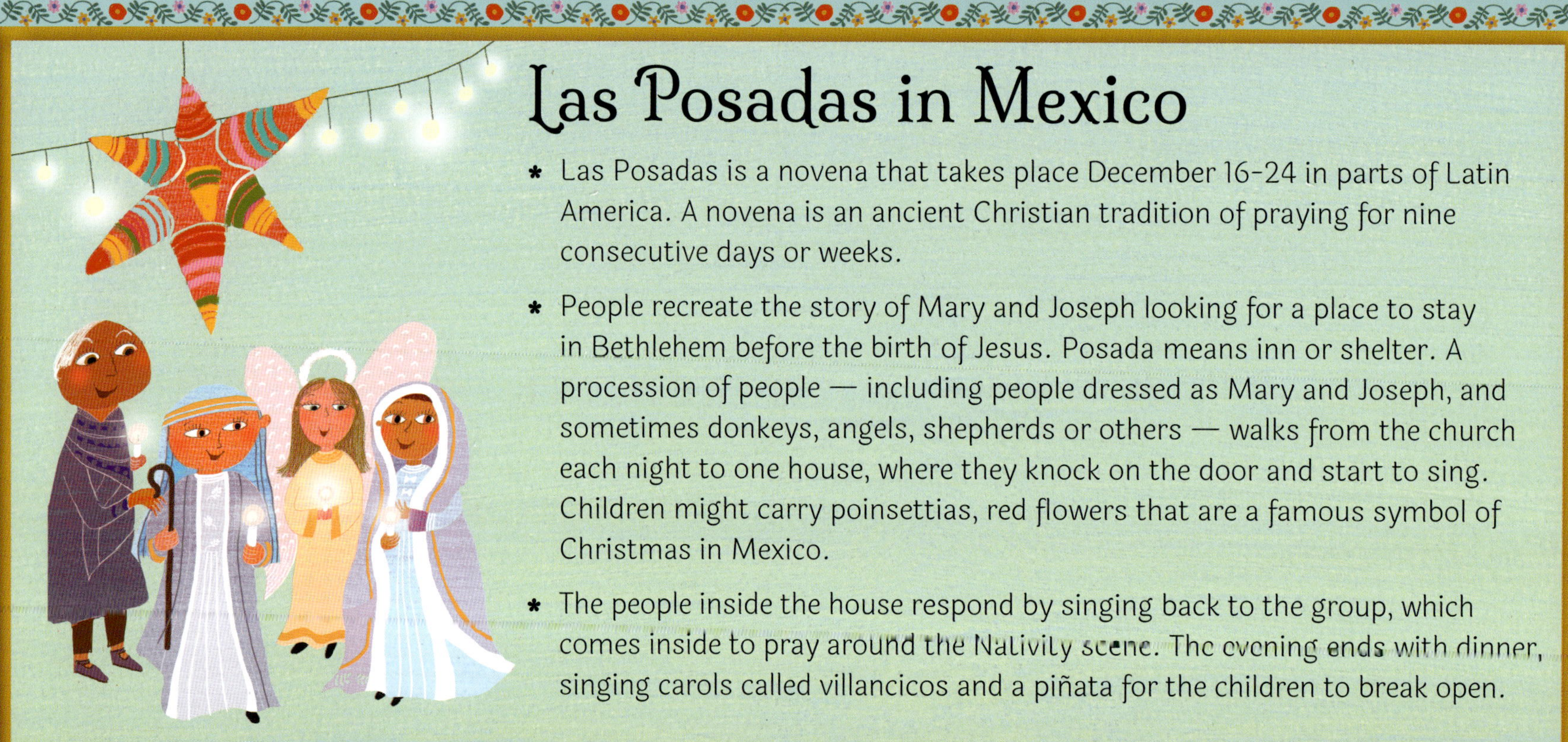

Las Posadas in Mexico

* Las Posadas is a novena that takes place December 16-24 in parts of Latin America. A novena is an ancient Christian tradition of praying for nine consecutive days or weeks.
* People recreate the story of Mary and Joseph looking for a place to stay in Bethlehem before the birth of Jesus. Posada means inn or shelter. A procession of people — including people dressed as Mary and Joseph, and sometimes donkeys, angels, shepherds or others — walks from the church each night to one house, where they knock on the door and start to sing. Children might carry poinsettias, red flowers that are a famous symbol of Christmas in Mexico.
* The people inside the house respond by singing back to the group, which comes inside to pray around the Nativity scene. The evening ends with dinner, singing carols called villancicos and a piñata for the children to break open.

Breaking Fast in Egypt

* Christians make up a small part of the population of Egypt and most Christians in Egypt are members of the Coptic Orthodox Church. They celebrate Christmas on January 7.
* For 43 days, everyone avoids eating foods that come from animals (meat, eggs and milk). When the Holy Nativity Fast ends, a lavish Christmas dinner is served with lots of foods that weren't eaten during the fasting. One popular dish is fattah, made from lamb, rice and bread.
* Christmas Eve is a time to dress nicely and gather together. Families might watch religious services on television after breaking their fast — Mass can last for several hours.
* Instead of gifts, older family members will present younger family members with money. Families might share kahk, a sweet biscuit, and drink tea on Christmas morning.

Genna in Ethiopia

* Ethiopia was one of the first regions in the world to officially adopt Christianity. In the Ethiopian Orthodox Church, Christmas is celebrated on January 7 and is called Genna.
* Most Christians fast for 43 days before Genna, eating simple meals only once a day with no meat, dairy, eggs or oil. Many break their fast with doro wot, a meat and vegetable stew served on top of thin, spongy injera bread. A honey wine called tej is also popular at Genna.
* Families eat around a basket-like table called the mesob. When the lid is removed, the mesob holds a feast for everyone to share. The practice of gursha is when one family member feeds another a large bite of food by hand.
* The preparation of coffee is a ceremony in Ethiopia, where it is said to have been first discovered. The beans are roasted fresh while incense burns. Then the coffee is poured carefully into small cups. Coffee is served at every special occasion.
* Ethiopia is known for a sport called Genna, which is similar to field hockey and played only at Christmas, but the tradition has become less popular in recent years.

Beach Picnic in Australia

* Australia is in the southern half of the world, so it is summer at Christmastime. Over 80% of Australians live on the coast. Many families like to eat their Christmas meal outdoors, because the beach is often the coolest place to be on a hot day.
* An Aussie BBQ often includes sausages, burgers, steaks and prawns. Bread and butter, a pile of grilled onions, an array of cold salads and plenty of sauces accompany the meal.
* People play cricket almost anywhere — at the beach, in parks, on the street or in their own backyards. While the meal is cooking, many families will grab their bats and balls and play!
* The Boxing Day Test is held the day after Christmas. It is one of the most anticipated cricket matches in the world and features the Australian cricket team and an international team. Tickets sell out months in advance!

Befana in Italy

* Epiphany is traditionally celebrated on January 6. In Western Christianity, Epiphany marks the day that the Magi, the Wise Men, visited the newborn Baby Jesus.
* According to Italian legend, an old woman named Befana was invited by the Wise Men to join them. She was busy with housework, so she stayed at home. The next day she tried to catch up but could not find them. Now she visits homes every year looking for the Baby Jesus.
* In Italy, on the night before Epiphany, Befana visits homes and fills stockings with sweets and gifts for children who have behaved and "coal" (which is really rock candy) for those who have not. Most children will receive both, because we all make mistakes!
* There are many poems and songs about Befana. One of the most popular ones exclaims, "Viva, viva la Befana!" which means, "Long live the Befana!"

Christmas Straw in Serbia

* Serbia has many unique Christmas traditions. In the Serbian Orthodox Church, the twelve days of Christmas are a time of prayer, worship and modest celebrations.
* Before Christmas Eve dinner, a badnjak is chosen and brought inside. A badnjak is an oak branch with its leaves still attached that is used in the fire on Christmas Eve. Once the badnjak has been collected and properly blessed, straw is scattered over the floor of the home.
* As the straw is spread, the grown-ups imitate hens saying "kvo kvo kvo!" and drop little treats on the straw. The children peep "piju piju!" like chicks and search for the treats.
* On Christmas Day, January 7, families attend church and share česnica, a sweet bread with a special coin hidden inside, and roasted meat, sauerkraut and other dishes.

Noche Buena in Argentina

* In Argentina, Christmas is celebrated in a grand way on Christmas Eve. Festivities begin with religious services in the evening.
* On Christmas Eve, Noche Buena, children dress up and act out the story of Christmas. These Nativity plays are performed outdoors because it is summertime and warm outside. At midnight the Baby Jesus is placed in his crib.
* Dinner is served late in the evening. Appetizers like tomates rellenos, empanadas and melon with prosciutto start the feast, followed by barbecued meats and cold dishes. A traditional dessert called pan dulce, a sweet bread filled with nuts and fruit, is enjoyed with ice cream cake and turròn, a sweet nougat mixed with peanuts or almonds.
* At the end of the night, celebrations continue with parties, presents, and in some places, fireworks at midnight! It's less common to see fireworks now, as the noise can be distressing to people and animals.

Christmas Book Flood in Iceland

* In Iceland, thirteen Yule Lads called Jólasveinar are said to visit each day until Christmas Eve, leaving little gifts in shoes. Each one has their own personality. If you misbehave, you'll find a raw potato instead of a treat!
* Because a book is often given during the thirteen days of gift-giving, many new books are published in Iceland just before the Christmas season. So many books are purchased that it's called a Christmas Book Flood, Jólabókaflóð!
* On Christmas Eve, a large meal is shared, complete with Christmas cookies called jólasmákökur. After dinner, families exchange gifts, then drink hot chocolate and read their new books together.
* Every Icelandic word about Christmas starts with "jól" because Jól is Icelandic for Christmas. To wish someone a Merry Christmas in Iceland, say, "Gleðileg jól!" (pronounced GLETH-leg YOHSH).

Nativity Scene in Lebanon

* The Middle East is the heart and home of three major religions — Christianity, Judaism and Islam. In Lebanon, Christians make up almost half of the population.
* Two weeks before Christmas, lentils or beans are prepared for sprouting. By Christmas, the little beans will grow into green sprouts to signify new life.
* Families work together to create a large Nativity scene in their homes. These works of art often show the entire city of Bethlehem surrounding a cave where Mary and Joseph rest. At midnight on Christmas Eve, Jesus is placed in the crib to symbolize his birth.
* In Lebanon, Baba Noël brings gifts to children, especially those most in need. He doesn't sneak in to hide gifts — he meets children face to face!

Author's Note

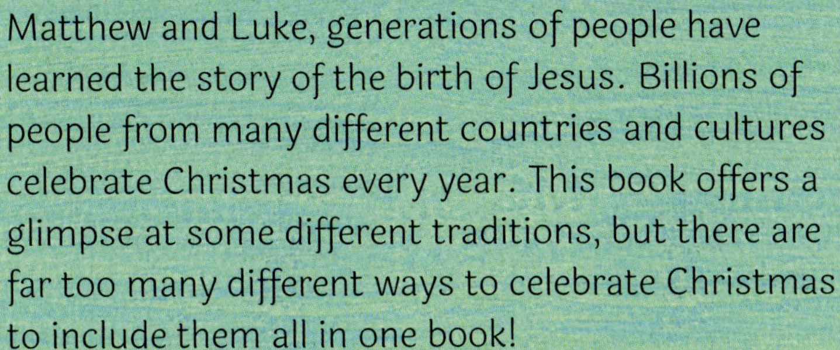

The story of Christmas comes mainly from two passages in the New Testament of the Bible. From these two short passages in the Gospels of Matthew and Luke, generations of people have learned the story of the birth of Jesus. Billions of people from many different countries and cultures celebrate Christmas every year. This book offers a glimpse at some different traditions, but there are far too many different ways to celebrate Christmas to include them all in one book!

Creating this book looked a lot like some of the scenes in this book — many people coming together to make something special. We collaborated with friends new and old from all 13 cultures represented in the book to make sure the words and pictures in this book tell an accurate and up-to-date story. The result is a feast for the senses, as rich and enjoyable as a Christmas dinner with all the trimmings. I am grateful to each of them for their help bringing this book to life — and grateful to each of you for reading it!

— Kate DePalma

Illustrator's Note

Illustrating this book brought back happy memories and helped me discover so many beautiful and charming Christmas traditions throughout the world.

When I was growing up in France, my dad used to make little oil lamps out of clementine peels at Christmas time. I love the mood of candles and being outside at night. It gives the sensation of being part of the universe. So it makes sense that, of all the exciting traditions in this book, I would most like to travel to Colombia for the Day of Little Candles.

Powerful sense memories of Christmas, like the sweet taste of a clementine, the smell of the tree and the glow of the lights, inspired me as I created the art for this special book. I created the illustrations using different media — acrylics, pencils, collage and even digital elements — to give the art richness, detail and depth. It was joyful to create and I hope it is joyful to read!

— Sophie Fatus

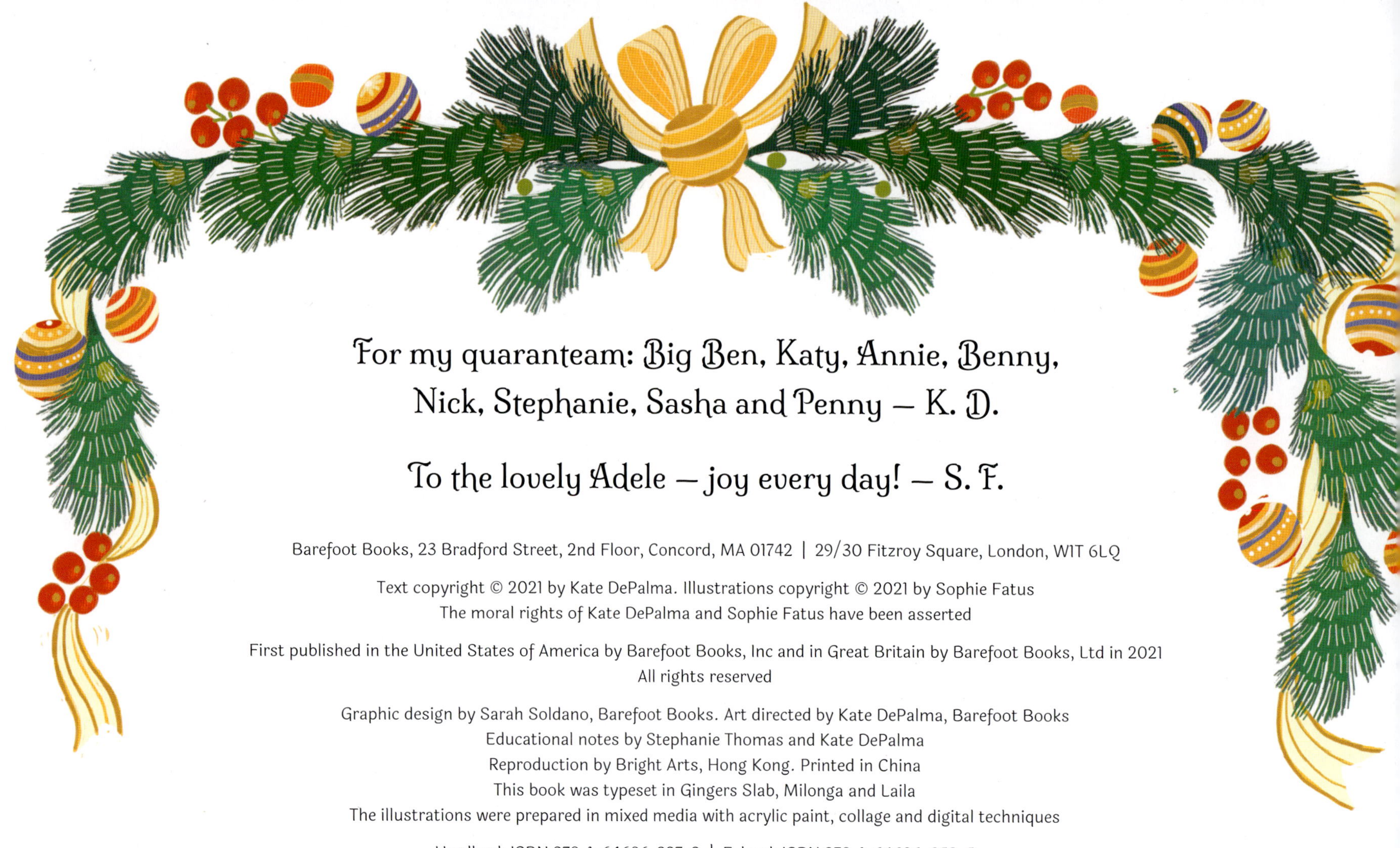

For my quaranteam: Big Ben, Katy, Annie, Benny, Nick, Stephanie, Sasha and Penny — K. D.

To the lovely Adele — joy every day! — S. F.

Barefoot Books, 23 Bradford Street, 2nd Floor, Concord, MA 01742 | 29/30 Fitzroy Square, London, W1T 6LQ

First published in the United States of America by Barefoot Books, Inc and in Great Britain by Barefoot Books, Ltd in 2021

Graphic design by Sarah Soldano, Barefoot Books. Art directed by Kate DePalma, Barefoot Books
Educational notes by Stephanie Thomas and Kate DePalma
Reproduction by Bright Arts, Hong Kong. Printed in China
This book was typeset in Gingers Slab, Milonga and Laila
The illustrations were prepared in mixed media with acrylic paint, collage and digital techniques

Hardback ISBN 978-1-64686-297-9 | E-book ISBN 978-1-64686-352-5

British Cataloguing-in-Publication Data: a catalogue record for this book is available from the British Library

Library of Congress Cataloging-in-Publication Data is available under LCCN 2021940379

5 7 9 8 6 4

The author is grateful to friends old and new from around the world who helped bring this book to life:

Sigurdur Adalgeirsson | Autumn Allen | Asunción del Azar de Etcheverry | Simon Botros
Sadeem El Nahhas | Marisel Mesa Gomez | Fitsum Habtemariam | Ana Lazarevi
Felani Merced | Jean Pierre Michel | Jen Mills | Rev. Dr. Nathan Parker | Natalie Power | Julia Reed
Ann Rollo | Sarahy Sigie | Wafa' Tarnowska | Stephanie Thomas | Melissa Wolff

Kate DePalma

loves making gingerbread houses, decorating the Christmas tree and reading "A Visit from St. Nicholas" aloud by the fire. She has written many books for children, including *Let's Celebrate: Special Days Around the World* and *Children of the World*, which she coauthored with Tessa Strickland. She lives with her family in Pittsburgh, Pennsylvania, USA.

Sophie Fatus

has warm childhood memories of making Christmas puddings in silly shapes and putting toy elephants inside her family's Nativity scene. She has illustrated many beloved Barefoot Books titles, including *Yoga Pretzels*, *If You're Happy and You Know It!* and *My Big Barefoot Book of Wonderful Words.* Sophie lives in Florence, Italy, with her partner and two cats.